IN THE ABSENCE OF CLOCKS

Crab Orchard Series in Poetry

Open Competition Award

Ukraine
Western Buh River
Chornobyl
Kyiv
Kharkiv
Lviv
Izyum
Dniper River
Vinnytsya
Ivano-
Frankivsk
Uman
Southern Buh River
Donetsk
Kherson
Odesa
Crimea
Black
Feodosiya
Simferopol
Sudak
Alushta
Sevastopol
Yalta
Sea

In the Absence of Clocks

JACOB SHORES-ARGUELLO

Crab Orchard Review
&
Southern Illinois University Press
Carbondale and Edwardsville

Printed in the United States of America

16 15 14 13 4 3 2 1

The Crab Orchard Series in Poetry is a joint publishing venture of Southern Illinois University Press and *Crab Orchard Review*. This series has been made possible by the generous support of the Office of the President of Southern Illinois University and the Office of the Vice Chancellor for Academic Affairs and Provost at Southern Illinois University Carbondale.

Crab Orchard Series in Poetry Editor: Jon Tribble
Open Competition Award Judge for 2011: Yusef Komunyakaa

Library of Congress Cataloging-in-Publication Data
Shores-Arguello, Jacob.
In the absence of clocks / Jacob Shores-Arguello.
p. cm. — (Crab Orchard Series in Poetry)
ISBN-13: 978-0-8093-3103-1 (pbk. : alk. paper)
ISBN-10: 0-8093-3103-9 (pbk. : alk. paper)
ISBN-13: 978-0-8093-3104-8 (ebook)
ISBN-10: 0-8093-3104-7 (ebook)
I. Title.
PS3619.H6657I5 2012
811'.6—dc23 2012011123

Printed on recycled paper. ♻
The paper used in this publication meets the minimum requirements of American National Standard for Information Sciences—Permanence of Paper for Printed Library Materials, ANSI Z39.48-1992. ♾

For my mother and my father

Contents

Acknowledgments ix

Finding the Old Family Farm 1

UKRAINE

In the Absence of Clocks 5
Crimea, an Unexpected Freeze 6
On the Holiday for the Dead 7
Graduation Day 8
The Dogs 9
Childhoods 10
The New Clock Tower 11
Secret Police 12
Babushka Baba Yaga 13
A Brief History of Ukraine 14

NORTH TOWARD KIEV

To Ukraine 17
Mapping the Republics of the Dead 18
Far South, an Unexpected Heat 19
The Danger in Leaving Her 20
Under the River Named God 21
Dear Father, 22
Bread 23
Mountain Answers 24
Remains 25
A Crumbling Shroud Covers Reactor Number 4 26
Some Pilgrimage 27

ORANGE REVOLUTION

Kiev 31

Revolution Comes to Kiev, Masha Comes to Kiev 32

Listening Device 33

Monument 34

The Orange Revolution 35

Masha in the Afternoon 36

Remember 37

Countrymen 38

Sex and the Orange Revolution 39

Baptism of Kiev 40

Revolution 41

BOUNDARY WATERS

Masha Back Home 45

Her Mother, Somehow Surprised 46

A New Economy, the Old Currency 47

Her Village, *Once Starved until All the Animals and All the Bullets Were Gone* 48

Ghost Sick 49

Violin and Sea 50

Untitled 51

Her Hair, Twin Braids of Dark Clove, 52

Paradise 53

Come Back 54

What I Saw 55

Finding the Old Family Farm II 56

Summer 57

Acknowledgments

Thank you to the editors of the following journals where some of these poems first appeared:

32 Poems: "Paradise"
Guernica: "Crimea, an Unexpected Freeze"
Indiana Review: "Listening Device," "Finding the Old Family Farm," "Graduation Day"

I am grateful to those individuals and institutions who made this book possible:

The Fulbright Program, The Fine Arts Work Center in Provincetown, Dzanc Books DISQUIET International Literary Program, Carolyn Walton, Davis McCombs, Michael Heffernan, John Duval, Geoffrey Brock, and everyone from the University of Arkansas Programs in Creative Writing and Translation.

Serhiy Vdovichenko, Susan Vdovichenko, Timber Massey, Vanessa Villava, Kyrylo Borodin, Maria Khmel'ova, Dmytro Malakhov

Yusef Komunyaka, Carolyn Forché, Jon Tribble, John Poch, Malachi Black, and Carolyn Guinzio

And to Chloe Honum, my deepest forever thanks.

IN THE ABSENCE OF CLOCKS

Чорне море ще всміхнеться, дід Дніпро зрадіє . . .

—Ще не вмерла Україна

The Black Sea will smile and grandfather Dnieper will rejoice . . .

—*"Ukraine Is Not Yet Dead," national anthem*

Finding the Old Family Farm

Near the Western Buh River, the traditional division between Catholicism and Orthodoxy, East and West

At dusk, I pole a split branch
through fog. This is old work,
as is my pitch-pine fire,

my mushrooms, borscht,
and smoked tea. Now the fields
grow only voices: ghost farmers

who shame the bloodless beets.
Redden, they say, *thrive.*

They pray into the breeze,
beneath the song of the stork,
the nightingale. From the hill's

heavy sickle of mist, the dead
still beg and bray. *The years
go on,* they say. What voice

can call back to these men,
answer the ox-hauled moon?

UKRAINE

In the Absence of Clocks

Vilor, the baker's son, sits on his stoop,
pours swept flour from one hand to the other.
A night of lightning has arrested the tower's
clockwork. Vilor waits to hear if it will
toll again. The dog-woman sleeps on the post-
office steps with her harem, their long fur twists
into her gypsy scarves. Vilor smokes. Knows
each day is made of four distinct chambers.
The dogs know nothing of time, they whimper
and wait for passersby to come with coins.
Vilor, the baker's son, dusts his hands.
Today, the village will be late for bread.
He stands. Night-music. It is very early—
the morning, a hollow space in his body.

Crimea, an Unexpected Freeze

A cold wolf hangs from the teat of upper
atmosphere. It sweeps the crags of coastline,

the dull smear of beach. Its breath cuts
through a cradle of rigging, the broad faces

of sails. The straw-boned seabirds are blown
from their trawlers, their religion of fish.

But the heavy pelicans remain, float
in the surprise of icewash, pick jewels

of freeze from wings, the feathery scissors
of their tails. As all warm animals do in Ukraine,

the pelicans try, but the long trowel of their beaks
cannot reach what is closest to them.

These great birds go last, too heavy to fly.
They sink under swelling breastplates of ice.

On the Holiday for the Dead

The whole village walks the hard pack
of arid steppe to the cemetery, to the river
where the ground is soft. The children do not
wait for the key, they slip between iron leaves,
a fencework of Orthodox crosses. They've all
brought bright woven blankets, blinchiky
with sour cream, and vodka. After they eat,
long shots are poured and left on the headstones
as gifts for the dead. Tomorrow, the children
will be sent to collect the empty glasses.
Careful, do not break these proofs of eternity.
Tonight, the old men will sneak back into
the cemetery, rob the grave-cooled spirits.
Make the old toast: *To childhood. To death.*

Graduation Day

The thin boy is a spy disguised by a magnolia—
an improvised trench coat. He blends in,
imagines his skin as bark. Through beetled
leaves, he watches the waterfall. Wet uniforms
peel from schoolgirls as they dance with the falls,
smoke, sing their vodka songs. The boy
is a good spy, knows every hair of these girls.
Except for Masha, the one who walks
in sleeves, rolled jeans, and tempts the water
with her toes. The lagoon is thirsty for her.
Brother Vladic yells for the boy: time to go,
plant potatoes for the imminent winter.
But the boy doesn't think in Februaries.
For him a year is a modest thing, naked to its ankles.

The Dogs

The old man's foot is a marionette that swings
from his crushed nub of knee. Divots of grass,
drags of gravel follow him as he hobbles
from the ticket men to the boys who guard
the mailbags. He asks for coins, for someone
in the village to please roll the tobacco he's found.
One day the man will have enough change,
take the first train that comes. No need to guess
what he will find. The boys have stolen letters,
they've read that in this country even the pines
are threshed by winter. A mutt who's robbed
the laundry plays on the iron tracks. The wind
breathes, the shirt whips. In this country, one sleeve
wraps around the dog's neck. Then another.

Childhoods

The girls' small almond eyes
tempt the flash from cameras.

These infants are the milk-faced
celebrities of the orphanage,

baby dolls sewn into delicate clothes.
People give only beautiful things:

thick ruffled dresses,
crocheted caps.

The older boys try to wrestle strangers,
do anything for touch.

The boys wear flowered wools,
girls shoes, exhausted lace.

In the visitor's chapel, the icon cradles
a Byzantine baby Jesus. The church's

paintings show the story of his future.
He hides his face in the virgin's neck.

The New Clock Tower

To see its thin iron arms
handle the hours
is to see the village's
new parade of boot traffic,
tires chewing up stones.
Before, this square held herds

of goats. Milk-heavy,
swaying, they dawdled among
the stalls of farmer's cheese,
fermenting kvass,
the ropes of lungfish
drying in the breeze.

Before it was emptied,
this place was animal.
Even now, flocks
of rock doves leave
their homes in the limestone,
flirt with the tower.

Six fat birds lumber
in the smoke-toned sky,
perch on the clock's
outstretched arm.
It bends, and
time is slow again.

Secret Police

Masha has seen them envelop the moon.
Do not ask what the crows have done.

Babushka Baba Yaga

Everything starts with frozen skulls
of cabbage that crack like lake ice,
ring the hollow of her iron pot.
The children outside her door
play the old game, imagine the sound
of marrow dropping in clots, fingers
bobbing to the top of her heavy soup.

She stops it with a slap of her axe
on the hard pack of snow.
Spitting streaks of steaming spiced wine,
she panics the tight jeer of children
until they break and scatter.
But Babushka Baba Yaga is not a witch.

She's a grandmother living in the grain shack:
a hut standing on four legs carved with
chicken feathers, leopard claws, spider web.
Totems against the desperation laced
into the eyelets of a remote village night.

A Brief History of Ukraine

In late evening, as the sundials died,
a storm of leaves forced color
onto the wind, revealed its spine.

Farmhands gave no notice
as the mountain air sucked clouds
from the valley. A milky fog collected
so thick it tasted on the tongue.
In this way a wolf could pass unnoticed
between a man and his self-loathing,
a child could be stolen from behind
the wall of his mother's love.
In the panic of this night,
ghosts were birthed from searchlights,
hounds discovered sirens in their throats.
By mid-morning the boy was found half-
alive near the dark leg of the Dnieper River,
deep in famine country.

The thin boy was woken each day after,
before even the liturgy of the rooster,
to tend the lamp of the sanctuary.

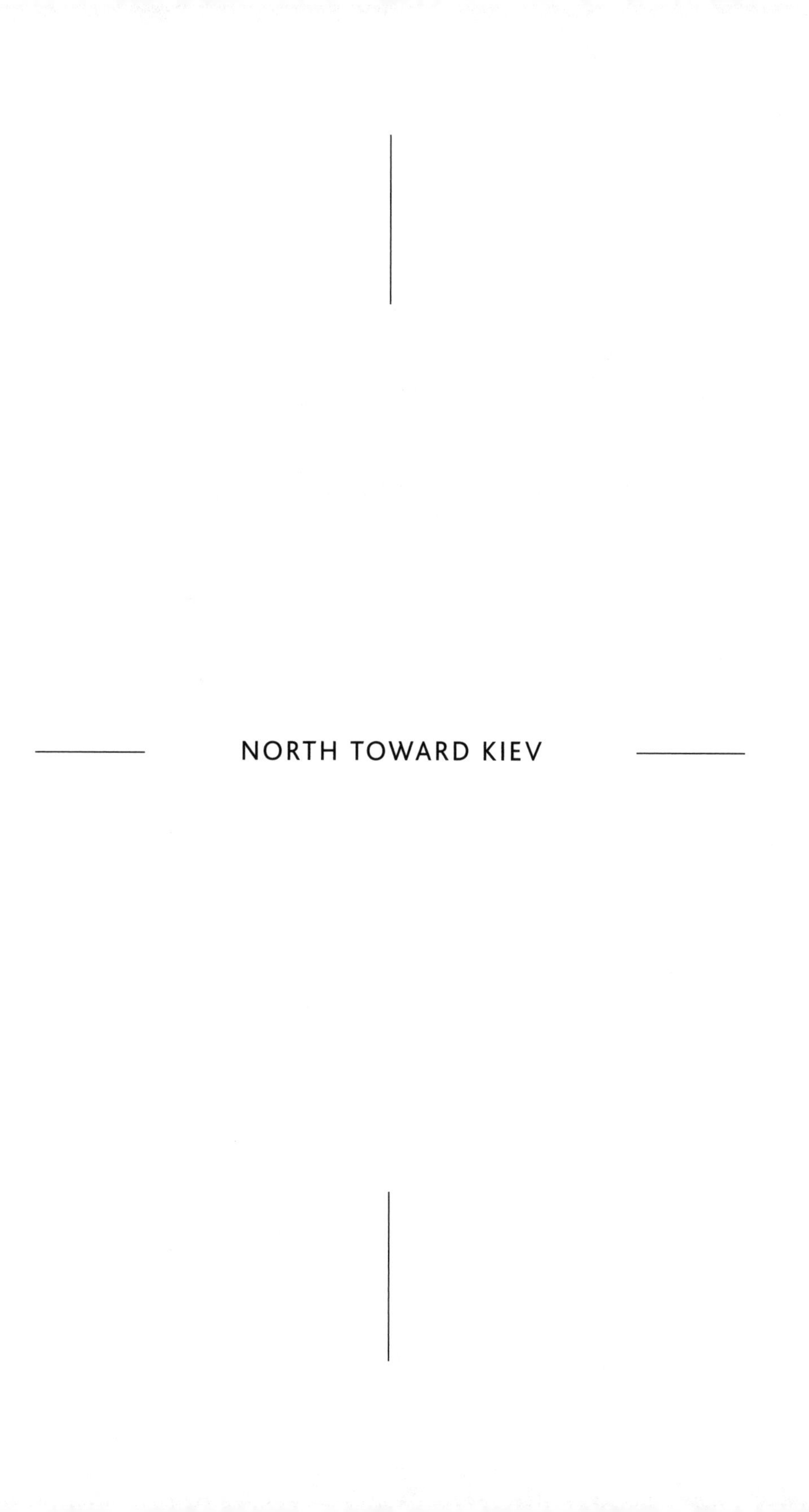

NORTH TOWARD KIEV

Any of the old countries that share latitude or soil with America has had a finger in its breadbasket.

—A. Schwartz

Kyiv is our city of baptism, beer, and revolutions. Some pilgrimage or another always ends up there.

— P. Bezimya

To Ukraine

On the Missouri River

A thin boy paces the fence-line surrounding
my parents' house. Inside, my father slowly

sickens, forgets his stories. When the boy leaves,
I follow. Farmers turn the coffee-dark soil

with huge machines, workers paint
the church white to match the moon. Soon,

the boy stops and turns, but heat has taken
the words he needs. We walk together.

He offers strange crosses, vodka bottles,
stalks of wild garlic. I balk, unsure if I am

the same as these things. *It is time for us
to go somewhere,* he finally says. Behind him,

naked girls play at baptism in the river,
the old paddle-wheeler is moored, ready.

And somehow, impossibly, a Cossack skiff.

Mapping the Republics of the Dead

Many children escaped occupied Ukraine,
but each in a different way.

Wadded silk blooms from the fisherman's hand,
an escape map, traced with blue, routes that match
the old man's wandering veins. *Here,* he points,
I was married. There, I harvested the winter's wheat.

The map is of a ghost country. The Black Sea
burns marine; it insists south, south, south.
At each village his finger stops. *Here, I lost my son.*
And here, my little dove, drowned. Beneath his finger,

the two-headed river is a monster. It quiets me.
But your silence is worse than any river, he laughs.
I tell him of the places my father has forgotten,
how I am to cross the country, north toward Kiev.

So, for this man you will map the republics of the dead?
He laughs again, offers me a cigarette and a caramel—
asks me to choose. The cigarette I think, but no,
look into his father-colored eyes. It's the caramel.

Far South, an Unexpected Heat

Crimea

No robes of snow to clothe the bare winter,
we lie in leftover fields, the unharvested cereals.
Masha smokes, hums to me: “Spring for Two
Violins,” “Ballet of the Unhatched Chicks.” We talk
about her early niece. How she fits neatly into
her grandmother’s cupped palm. Above hops
and flowering rye, a bittern makes knots
in the too-warm sky. A spider tunes his brief life,
stretches string across pine. All things plying
their extra time. I leave Masha. The bittern
calls. A finger of thistle points at the moon.
In the early morning, I collect a wanderer’s
bouquet: the wine grapes, pomegranates, figs.
Go north. Winter, demise, these necessary things.

The Danger in Leaving Her

Tattooed onto the slim epic of Masha's body, the Dante:
LASCIATE OGNE SPERANZA, VOI CH'INTRATE.

Under the River Named God

Vinnitsiya

A bunker was built for Hitler near the Southern Buh River
out of cursed rock. It was meant as a slow assassination,
a tomb for the end of the war.

The groom took only the men.
Crucified to the deck by nails
of vodka, we sang and did little else.
The river conducted our escape,
spun the wedding boat in witless circles.

As we beached on a hillock of cherries,
the bare trees of worship, I forced
myself to follow. The hills flowered
with smoke. The dirt began to flake
into brittle yellow teeth.

A riveted trapdoor was pried
so we could wander the tunnels
carved from *witch's rock.*
We found copper shells and radio wire.
A face that could not be seen

asked me where I was from, then why
I had come so far. Under the river
named God, a torch lit the graffiti,
the Cyrillic rock: *Radioactive, Without Escape.*
Things he knew I could not understand.

Dear Father,

I know you are scared for me,
but in Horlivka,
it is not like you have heard.

The beer still tastes like beer.
The girls who serve it
still trust their hips, like girls.

True, the birds you notice
are not like birds. They are soot
and cinder. Spastic blacks,

panics of sky. In Horlivka, 13 doves
sit on factory wires and blacken.
The 14th, a Crimean white, alights.

Bored with leisure, he settles
into the work of the town, turns to coal.
I know you are scared for me.

Bread

Lviv

Outside the dacha where I sleep,
I follow the mud, the gooseprints

that lead to the table. Babushka brings
bread and salt. If we have nothing,

we will always have bread and salt—
a psalm of communism and wars.

She cooks long shoots of chive,
mushroom spice, a storm of oil.

I eat and eat. Onions, pig-fat,
black bread. Later I will be taken

to the new church, the lavish
missionary's table. He is American

and a believer. I bring onions,
salted bread tucked in my pockets.

Mountain Answers

Ivano-Frankivsk

In the valley, elk leave long grooves in the hardpack,
a labyrinth solved by falling snow.

The cabins wait for avalanche, start their fires.
Smoke escapes, white columns torn

by wind: ghost-cranes in a birdless sky.
Finally, the far city becomes nothing

but the bones of its lights. Between whiteouts,
I watch the beaten peak—

What part of me needs this demise?
I wait as the burdened mounds of summit-drift

bulge, pile, climb. There was never any remedy,
there was never any reply.

Remains

In the salt rock catacombs of Slavyansk,
the ghost-monks play games of durak on carved
chalk tables. The walls are lined with candlelight
and their small bodies. *Shriveling trinkets,* they say,
shy bone dolls. In the belowground, no one

knows of the morning cicadas, their sharpening
knives of song. My escape into this Monument
of Sacred Caves is blocked by a brace of monks,
an aspergillum of Easter willow whips baptismal
waters across my face. The monks take my hands,

fold two fingers, strip my chest. A thumbnail
scores into my skin. Byzantium's cross: a head
to belly slice, right to left across the heart.
Deep, we let the catacombs prowl around us.
With raw vodka tongues, we play cards.

It is told that the sky is an unraveling tapestry
tugged on by the needles of the pine.
The sun, a heathen. In the belowground,
all that remains is compact, quiet, considered—
held by a stub of wax, a flicker.

A Crumbling Shroud Covers Reactor Number 4

Chernobyl

The blackening villages do not speak
of the sarcophagus: the fatigued concrete dome
that shields the restless neutrinos. I get no answer
when I ask about the reactor, if I should drink
the water, if it's true that mushrooms soak
radiation from the soil. I see the way they sip tea,
saw flanks of truffle-fattened boar meat.
Their steady hands reveal nothing of *fallout,*
collapse. But the yellowing signs on the roads
do speak: they say that no one lives in the Zone
of Exclusion. In the Zone of Exclusion, we drink
the curative herbs steeped in liquor. As meat
and wormwood are shared, no one lives. Lifeless,
we drink heavy. Drink with radiant ease.

Some Pilgrimage

Into Kiev

Each step is measured in a note of the wren.
We count miles by his song, sleep among

the beds of *solemn little children,* another name
for fields of glowing poppy. It cannot

be explained: the river frozen, hard as hourglass,
its path cut through the soft belly of spring.

Spores of milkweed collect in the wind,
sew themselves into a curtain of lace.

I write home to my father, tell him that this place
is no kin to memory. It hardens, cannot unravel

with time. Although he does not answer, I hold
his response in my chest. Hoping for water,

we all reach the Church of the Tithes together.
One by one, we step across the impossible river.

ORANGE REVOLUTION

This Revolution
is rebirth, is freedom,
is something . . .

—Graffito, perhaps unfinished, on
Independence Square, 2004

Water your new liberty
With blood for rain.

—Taras Schevchenko, 1844

Kiev

The dog does not know the city
outside this city, or the world
outside this world.

The baker *thwacks*
his broomstick against cement
to drive the dog away.

The baker knows some
of the city outside this city,
some of the world
outside this world.

I buy my bread.
I know nothing of this city,
but some of the world
outside this world.

The dog follows me.
With no one else to talk to,
I let him.

The dog cares nothing
about cities outside of cities,
or worlds outside of worlds.
He lives without boundary

in the universe of my shoes,
and the bread:
the bread inside of the bread,
the bread inside of the dog.

Revolution Comes to Kiev, Masha Comes to Kiev

We spoke nothing of the poisoning,
the ruined face of Ushenko
who drank deeply the waters of death.

Instead, we rowed to the river's middle,
started work. Our silt-backed island grew
beneath us as the water withdrew, gave birth

to lonely country. Our sanctuary
we plastered with horsehair and quicklime
snuck via the Dnieper by the night-sailers

who glided in like a hushed wedge
of oily swans. We built our claim quickly,
hammers hardening to monuments in the cement.

In the streets, revolution was collecting in clots.
Soon there would be no place to walk.

Listening Device

We disturb the Dnieper's delicate music with skipped
cod bones. Masha convinces a fisherman to lend
his rowboat. I open up sparkling wine, pistachios,
the same three chords on a borrowed guitar. Earlier,
the strange matchbox we found in Masha's mattress
was a joke, little wire antennas like a cockroach.
At least someone listens to you, I laughed. Now, we spin
in an undergrowth of magnolias, a thick grove
of shadows, and we growl. We spit. Heave bottles
into the water—glass more substantial than bone.
Silence pretends to be a passive thing. *Speak no words
you would not speak to God,* Masha says. Betrayed
by quiet, we do not pray to darkness. We demand.

MONUMENT

> *Being able to forget will be Kyiv's*
> *only monument to war.*
>
> —*P. Bezimya*

A thin boy stands at the ravine
of Babyn Yar, like a monument.

He is long black hair.
He is not a monument,

but soft and new
as independence.

If he were bronzed,
his plaque would read:

33,771–

a specific number of people,
a systematic kind of gunfire.

The thin boy stands at the ravine
of Babyn Yar, like a monument.

He is long shag coat,
but this is not Babyn Yar.

The boy, my guide, has gotten lost
in the music of his headphones.

This ravine is a monument
to nothing but ravines.

The Orange Revolution

Built as a sanctuary from bombs,
the Kiev Metro is the deepest in the world.

A long metal catheter
radiates through the city—
subway cars cry and shudder
reckless as water.
Hesitating to a stop,
we close in on *Schevchenko,*
pick up orange-clad protestors.
Sparrows play in the buried sky,
nest in frescoes, ignore the painted
sun. At *Independence Square*,
we dance and we drink. At *Obolon*, the crowds
shout of poison, of faces scarred
by dioxin. At *Dnieper*, the final stop,
the last of the passengers drain
out toward the river. I wait for the fluorescents
to flutter. Just me, and a man
shielding his baby. A boy who sleeps here
because here is where he sleeps.
The child coos; I wait. For the train
to die. For the train
to start again.

Masha in the Afternoon

The pocket watch demanded
bare skin.

Masha fought against her
frost-stiff gloves,

pulled with her teeth
so she could finger

the milk-washed inlays,
its glassy tranquility.

Human bone, the gypsy said.
Whose?

she asked him. And *when?*

Remember

Poor-man's cherub, the thin boy
flies by modest means,
balloons tied to his ears.

Me, with a lassoed pair of moths.
Our low altitude allows a closer watch
on the odd celebrations:

memorial days with no men,
women dancing with women.
Widows who brooch themselves

in the silvers and ribbons of war,
remnants of the generation of men
who should be dancing.

Strange, the boy says,
Why wear a dead man's medal?
His answer flushes across

a dancer's cheek. A presence
is marked, a swirl of blackbirds
fingerprints the sky.

Countrymen

Masha bloodies the pickpocket with a flagpole.
Don't you know that we're brothers now? We're whole?

Sex and the Orange Revolution

From our bed, we can hear the crowds
stomp and chant. Masha fights out of her orange
clothes, anchors her knees to my hips. I truss her
with sheets, tell her that she must sleep, that I
must go. At the corner bar, the men speak of nothing
but poison, the bartender's smile is the yellow
of worn piano keys. He knows everything.
Tells me how the city allows no one to forget
or leave. Outside, the protesters' moon is a plate
of bruised fruit, the air is chilled by a boy's violin.
I walk, not knowing where. Only later do I notice
how Masha's door moans, how she doesn't hear.
Her sleeping eyes undress only for the streetlight,
live and orange behind me.

Baptism of Kiev

Open to the arrows of snow, the crowds yowl
beneath our window, attempt to heat the air with song.
Masha thinks we sleep still, like fish in an icy pond.

But I brood, flinch as boys hurl tomatoes at bricks.
They cheer when the thin blood falls. A loudspeaker
hisses how we must change, *leave our corruptions behind.*

Soon the snow-washed sky begins to burn.
Even as the orange sun boasts of another revolution,
not all of what we are falls away. Good fear

presses its thumbs into my eyes. On Masha's cheek,
I trace a thin scar, a hidden crack in a new bowl.

Revolution

Palm Sunday, pussy willow. Through the trolley's
window I watch the flower girls sell. Men and women
hold stems. The downy unborn flowers are snow-
storms in miniature. *Why the willow?* I ask.
The mountains sharpen their snowy chisels against
the sky. A carriage horse, blazed white, stamps
through a pine-lit park. *Because palms do not grow
this far north.* By Easter, the trolley-stops fill again.
Now, the girls wave icons, cry *Poppies, Carnations*.
As a boy, I was taught only of the famously changed:
seventeen-year cicadas, St. George's salamander,
the medusas, and polyps of jellyfish. I didn't know
that the palm becomes the willow, this far north.

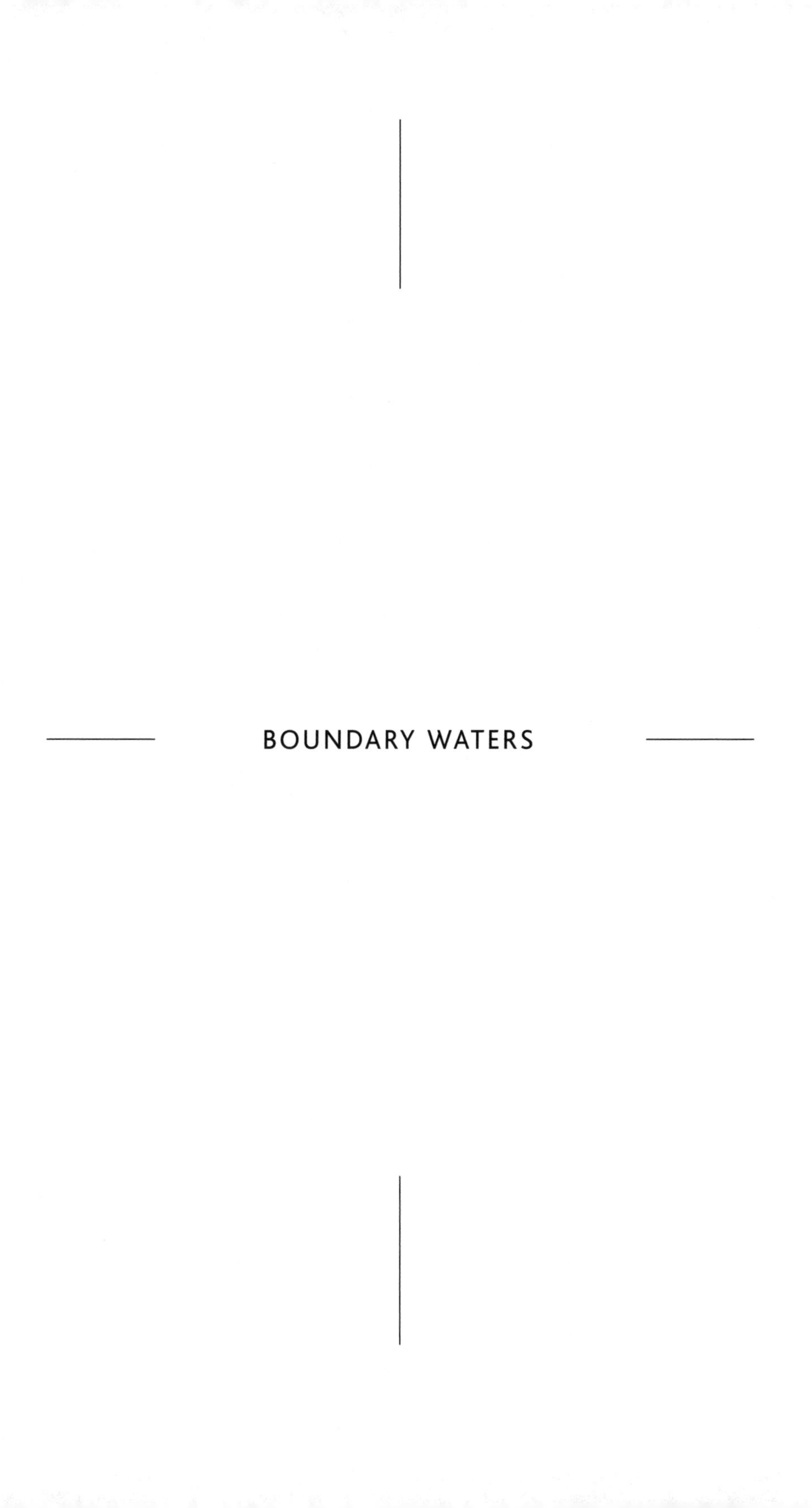

BOUNDARY WATERS

Україна Ukra · yi · na

Rus. lit. "the borderlands,"
from u- "at" + krai "edge."

Маша Ma · sha

diminutive of Maria/Miryam (Heb.)
of uncertain origin
perhaps meaning "beloved,"
perhaps meaning "sea of bitterness."

Masha Back Home

All of Crimea speaks of fresh water
in the past tense. Still the mourners try:

they drip candle wax like rain—it hardens
to stars in the black sky of their shoes.

The sidewalk boys drink their vodka,
raise their *little water* to the dead.

Days in the dry country, we take
to walking through fields of stones.

At her father's grave, Masha feels nothing.
Looking at the sky: *cloudburst will kill us both.*

Her Mother, Somehow Surprised

that Masha was a child of winter. The heat,
she was sure, would be her first language.

Unbelievable, she shares over dried herring
and fisherman's tea, *that my girl is no cousin*

to these waters. I tell her one of my father's stories,
of a lost fawn, sequined with ice, splayed

on a frozen pond. I describe its rescue:
the Guard helicopter lowering, the fat fingers

of wind pushing the deer to a shoulder of snow.
As we laugh, Masha enters the room, searches

the cupboards. *Impossible* that she will speak to us.
We sit unobserved—silence, a frost that sticks

until we are white as air, alone. We, the lost
ones here. *The girl, a climate all her own.*

A New Economy, the Old Currency

A sudden, new kind of job. *We will sell medicine*
to the hospital, Masha says. Everything that is white
is green: tinted by weak light, the walls become
wings of a luna moth. The patients in wheelchairs
sit in a circle. I ask a woman where
she was born. She speaks only about windows, doors.
Outside, we hear two dogs growl. Then whine.
A normal breath, the woman whispers to an old man
with girl-soft skin. Inside the office, the doctor asks
questions that no one can answer. My breath quivers.
Masha walks to his desk, bends. Even from behind,
I know the scallops of lace, the crescent of moon-
rinsed skin. A furtive white. The green undone.
Always there, between a second and third button.

Her Village, *Once Starved until All the Animals and All the Bullets Were Gone*

Overlooking the old village, Masha eats the kidney quietly. Like prayer.
My grandfather, she says, *was the first to grab a pigeon from the middle of the air.*

Ghost Sick

Inside the reindeer-skinned sweat lodge,
steam is the medicine for clarity. Solid blooms
of white rise from aloe-splashed rocks.
In the forest, a woodpecker works his piston.
Roots freeze, unfreeze, flex like arthritic fingers.
A half-wolf howls. Masha and I sing the only song
we both know, "Ukraine Is Not Yet Dead,"
the national anthem. We dance in the cold,
drink honey-pepper vodka. As we lash each other
with birch branches, the large dog steps from
the evening's dark hem. He growls. Real.
But there is medicine for fear. We scream—
run instead from a cloud of moths. Our dead we think,
their souls flying by. The dog left behind.

Violin and Sea

The moon's face still splashed with sea water,
I leave the reef. Cloak myself in low hanging trees,
the swells of crimson fruit. Somewhere, Masha saws
at the violin. The songs I do not know sound like
wild strawberries. Blueprints of coral still pressed
into the soles of my feet, I watch the beach, trace
the path of a fallen frond as it minuets with the sea.
A year ago we were creatures of this tide, let currents
steal us from the coastline. On our air mattress,
we made love on the water, awoken by blood wasps,
the ruffled whips of jellyfish. In this hidden dacha,
I groan: *Masha, come watch this palm with me.*
She practices an old song—a seabird's shadow
spirals from nowhere, hangs flightless on her face.

Untitled

This is all there is—
a sky of flint and steel.

Lying on their backs,
they talk too loud, say

that peels of palm bark
are locks of the girl's hair.

That Saturn must hulk
over its empire of moons.

She asks again about his
father's health,

his quiet sermon on forgetting.
In this way it is easy to say

nothing new, leave their revolutions
untended. She says that tonight

she'd rather sleep in a bed
with her sister, in her father's

old room. Some evenings,
smog and rain will mix, burnish

the machines of the sky,
a tremendous blaze of orange.

As she leaves—
a sky of flint and steel.

Her Hair, Twin Braids of Dark Clove,

listless hookah smoke.
A scent still woven into the air,

dyed into the Tatar curtain.
Moonlight unspools though the keyhole,

the abandoned bed blooms mimosa.
The open door frames nothing,

drapes hang like empty sleeves.
The note she left on the desk:

Crimea can never be enough,
beauty is not a kind of sustenance.

Paradise

Odessa cannot hide from itself. The waves
glance off the shoreline. The shipyard cranes
work slowly, separate what is not sea from the sea.
The bread, baked without molasses. The soup,
white with kefir. Alone, I sit in a café stirring
cream into coffee. I don't know what to say
when the waiter slides next to me. Eventually,
I admit my stories. The girl I met on this beach,
our revolution in the streets of Kiev. The man
finds vodka. Slaps down pickles, bowls of pistachios.
How do you know that Adam and Eve were communists,
he asks. His laughter foams like the sea, cannot
hide from itself. *Because they had no clothes to wear,*
no sausage to eat, and still they thought it was paradise.

Come Back

My cut lip sewn by a stranger's unsteady hand,
stitches crawling from my skin, black legs

of a centipede. Here in Café Odessa Steps,
I order a *usual,* ask where to find my friend.

He is the empty chair at our table, his father says.
I look at the insolent sea, touch my lip. *Marooned,*

I think. *Unbrothered.* But the sunset water is the color
of mulled wine; it reminds me of my own father.

One must be a priest of anything, he would say,
a priest of leaves. I tell the man *not now, but soon.*

How his son will come back. How boys always do.

What I Saw

For Father

A metal rainbow straddles the city
like a horseman's bowed legs. The monument
is bled of refraction, color. I feed kopeks
into the tourist scope and pan away.

A boy manufactures reams of delight
from nothing. A woman invades the frame
selling knots of garlicked bread, tied warm
like the twist on a newborn's belly.

Boy to Woman:
You are transparent and sing a clumsy song.
Woman to Boy:
But don't you know how I planted you?

Misread Ukrainian lips—I am
inaccurate. Through the lens, the moon
distends, a long silver oval.
Wrong and beautiful.

Finding the Old Family Farm II

Near the Western Buh River, the traditional division
between Catholicism and Orthodoxy, East and West

On the river, a black snake cuts water,
ripples on a farmer's brow. I kneel to caress
the green necks of soybeans. Fingers of light
tear through their leaves. The thin boy, my guide,
affixes paper to a cross. A scarecrow's shadow
stretches across the field, black loam shaping
from the plow. The boy says how this farm
was once a quarry. Churches as far as Warsaw
will remember these fields. As Masha bathes,
the river named God drags between countries.
The boy says that I am free to walk her westward,
over the boundary water—take her home.
I have no more questions. The boy's kite rises.
Yellow and blue, it's all that holds back the sky.

Summer

Heavy seabirds
fly low. The evening sun,
a sunken skiff,

means less to them
than the fish,
the fishermen

who brace themselves
against the pull
of the dim waters.

If I were younger,
I would turn
to Masha,

convince her
of the ocean's
old deaths.

Of life's
brief island.

If older,
I might worry
divinity.

But I am
neither.
We never are.

Other Books in the Crab Orchard Series in Poetry

Muse
Susan Aizenberg

Lizzie Borden in Love: Poems in Women's Voices
Julianna Baggott

This Country of Mothers
Julianna Baggott

The Black Ocean
Brian Barker

The Sphere of Birds
Ciaran Berry

White Summer
Joelle Biele

Rookery
Traci Brimhall

In Search of the Great Dead
Richard Cecil

Twenty First Century Blues
Richard Cecil

Circle
Victoria Chang

Consolation Miracle
Chad Davidson

The Last Predicta
Chad Davidson

Furious Lullaby
Oliver de la Paz

Names above Houses
Oliver de la Paz

The Star-Spangled Banner
Denise Duhamel

Smith Blue
Camille T. Dungy

Beautiful Trouble
Amy Fleury

Soluble Fish
Mary Jo Firth Gillett

Pelican Tracks
Elton Glaser

Winter Amnesties
Elton Glaser

Strange Land
Todd Hearon

Always Danger
David Hernandez

Heavenly Bodies
Cynthia Huntington

Red Clay Suite
Honorée Fanonne Jeffers

Fabulae
Joy Katz

Cinema Muto
Jesse Lee Kercheval

Train to Agra
Vandana Khanna

If No Moon
Moira Linehan

For Dust Thou Art
Timothy Liu

Strange Valentine
A. Loudermilk

Dark Alphabet
Jennifer Maier

Lacemakers
Claire McQuerry

Oblivio Gate
Sean Nevin

Holding Everything Down
William Notter

American Flamingo
Greg Pape

Crossroads and Unholy Water
Marilene Phipps

Birthmark
Jon Pineda

Threshold
Jennifer Richter

On the Cusp of a Dangerous Year
Lee Ann Roripaugh

Year of the Snake
Lee Ann Roripaugh

Misery Prefigured
J. Allyn Rosser

Roam
Susan B. A. Somers-Willett

Huang Po and the Dimensions of Love
Wally Swist

Persephone in America
Alison Townsend

Becoming Ebony
Patricia Jabbeh Wesley

A Murmuration of Starlings
Jake Adam York

Persons Unknown
Jake Adam York